Y0-BLS-119

Descendants

3

Bobby Guzman

Mal

Carlos

Hades

Jay

Gil

Uma
UmA

harry hook

harry hook

Dizzy

Evie

Celia

DESCENDANTS

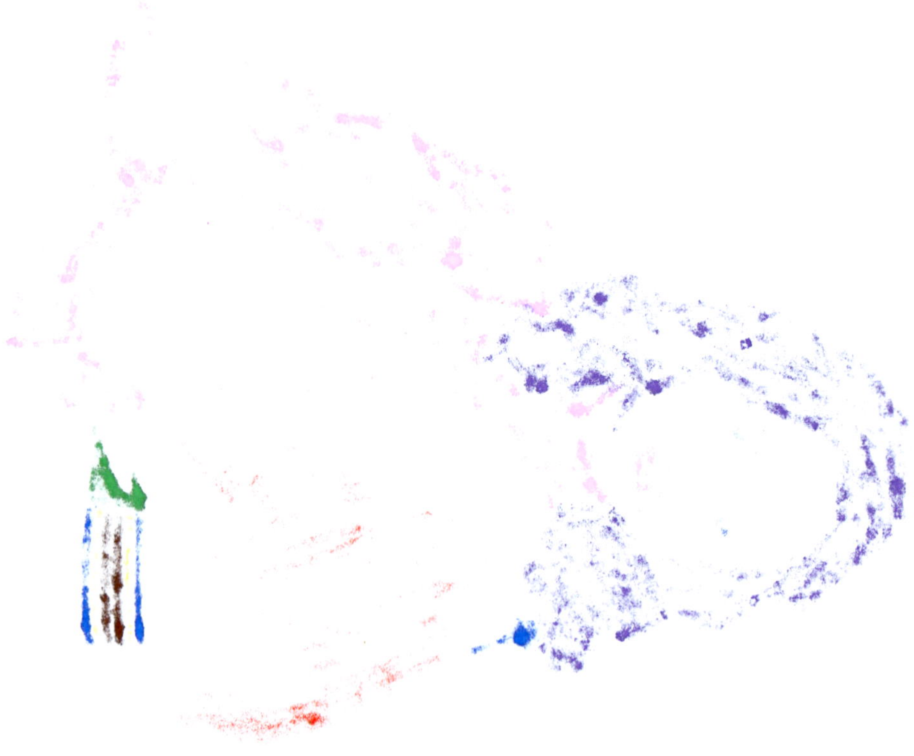

AURADON

DESCENDANTS 3

DESCENDANTS 3

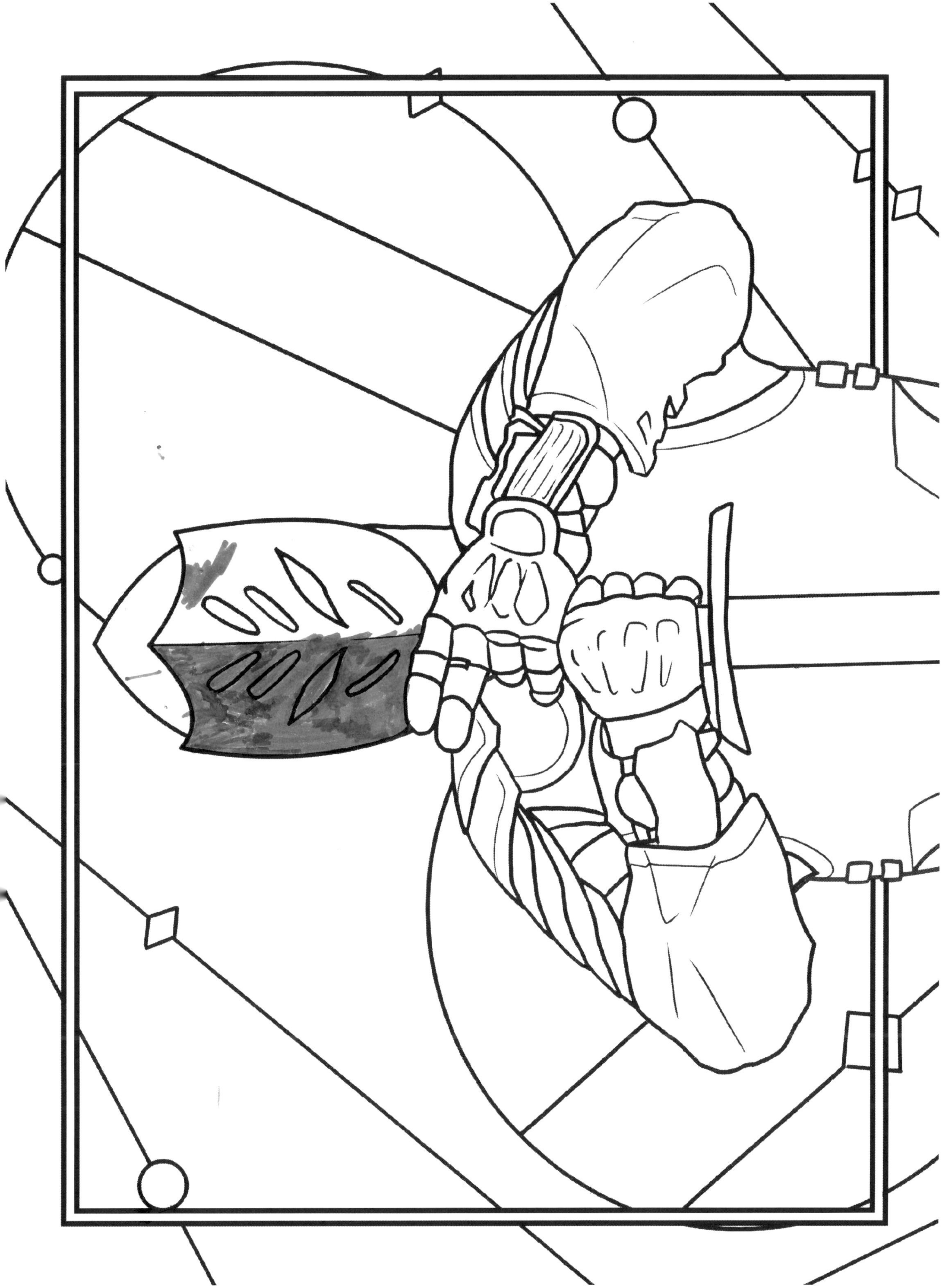

Audrey

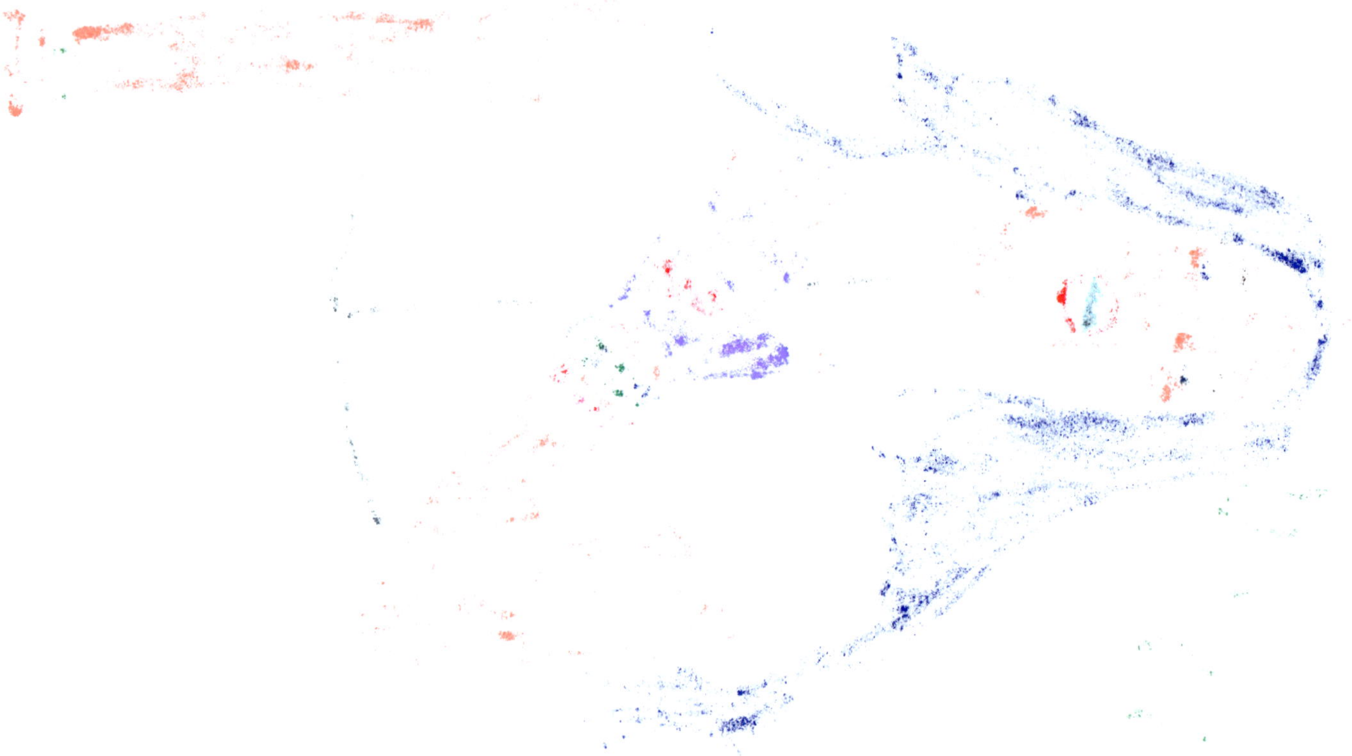

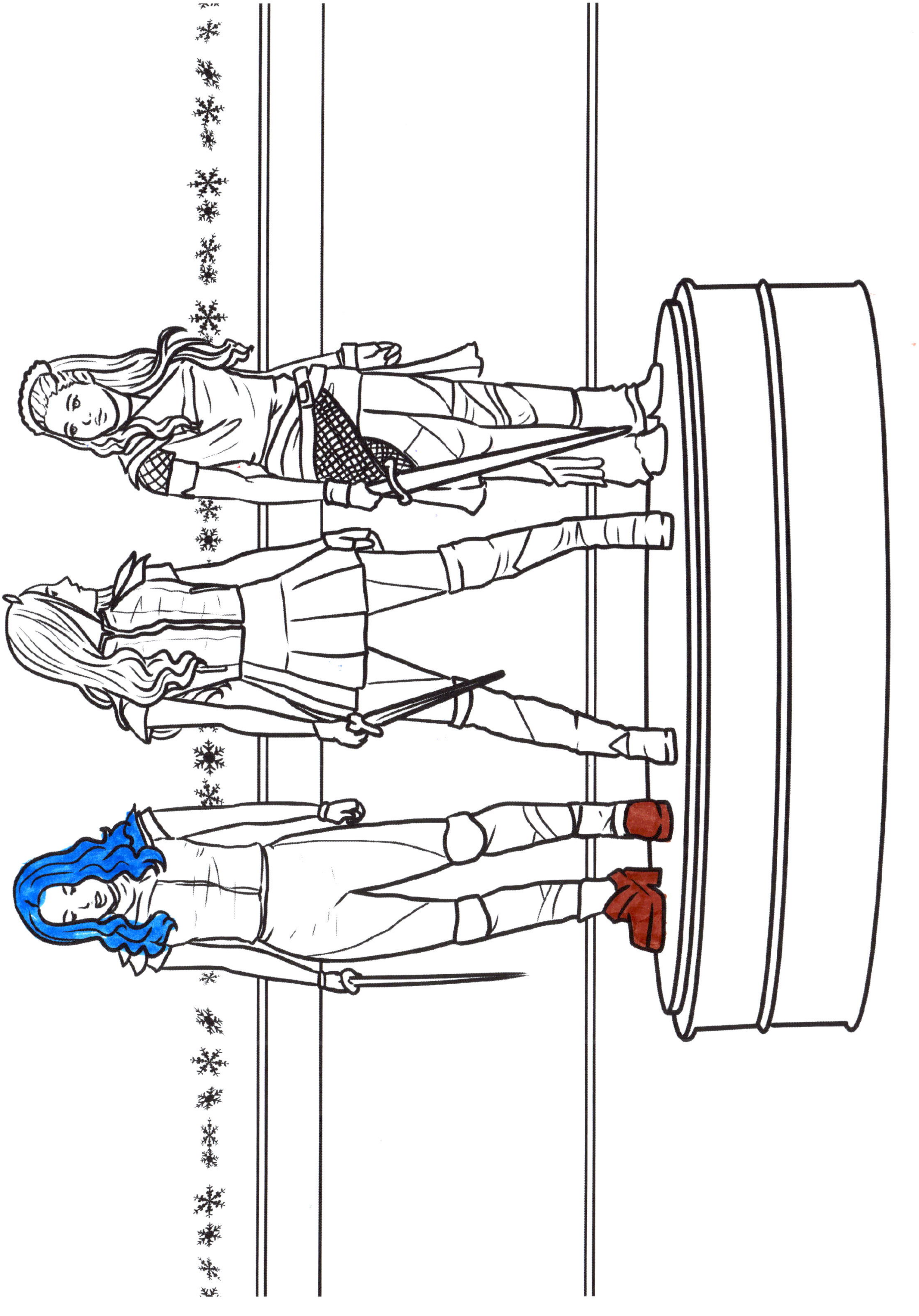

Ben

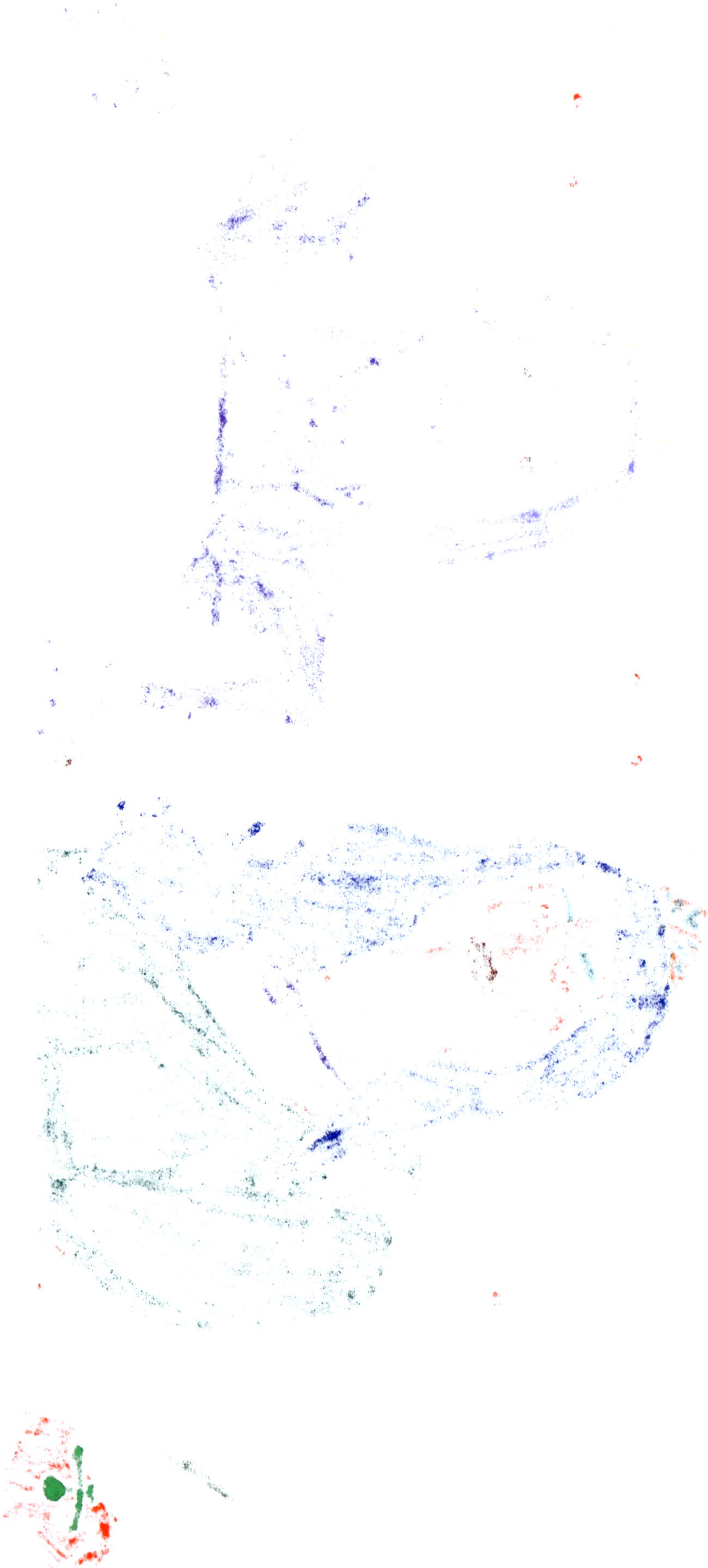

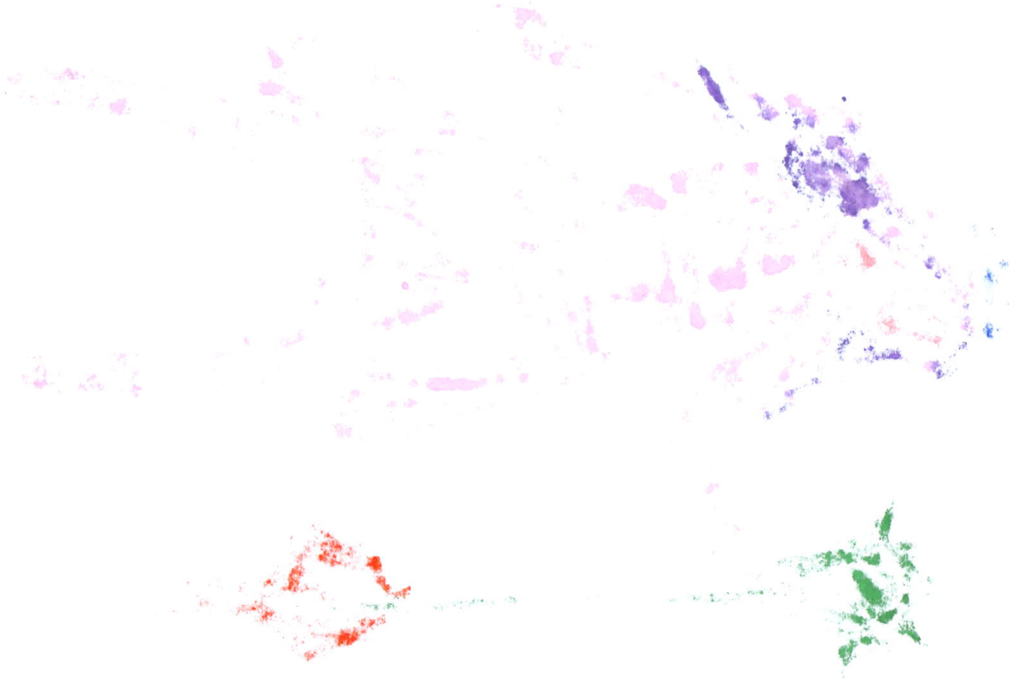

DESCENDANTS 3

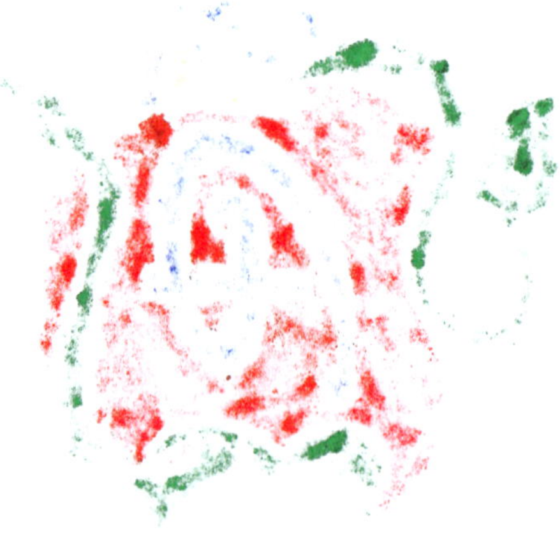

calors
erie
mal
jay

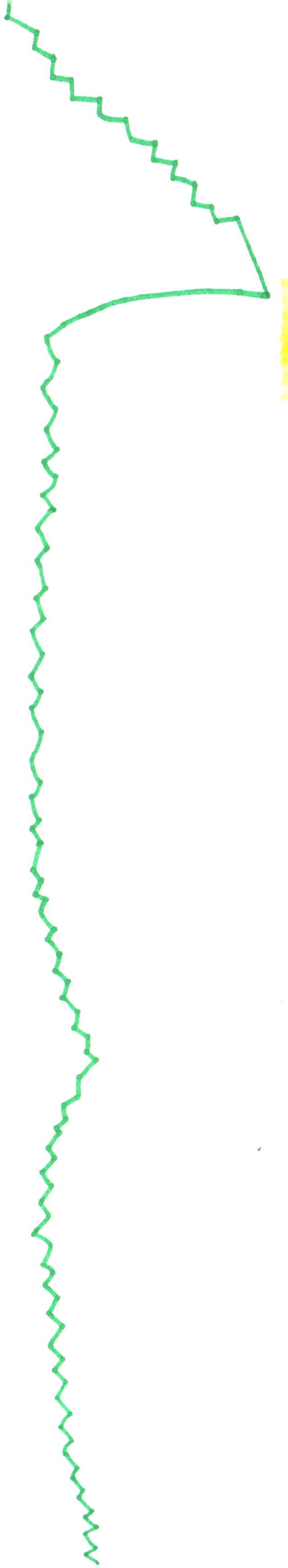

Made in the USA
Middletown, DE
02 December 2019

79716231R00040